THE LANGUAGE OF LEADINGS

The language of leadings

A REFLECTION ON FAITH, ACTION AND CONCERN

Jane Pearn

First published July 2017

Quaker Books, Friends House, 173 Euston Road, London NW1 2BJ

www.quaker.org.uk

ISBN 978 1 907123 98 6
eISBN 978 1 907123 99 3

Book design by Cox Design, Witney

Cover photo by Jane Pearn

"It takes great confidence to tackle unfamiliar tasks;
failing confidence, it takes great trust, and hope,
and willingness to make mistakes."

Christine Davis, *Minding the future* (Swarthmore Lecture), 2008, p. 32

CONTENTS

ACKNOWLEDGEMENTS

I am grateful to Woodbrooke Quaker Study Centre for awarding me an Eva Koch scholarship and so providing me with six weeks in which to think, reflect and learn. I felt supported by the helpfulness and kindness of Martin Layton and all the staff, and of the Friends in Residence: the atmosphere they create sustained me. Countless conversations about 'concern' with Friends as they came and went deepened my understanding. Especial thanks are due to Simon Best for his encouragement and suggestions, and to Angela Kyte, Brenda Heales, Kate Green and my fellow Eva Koch scholars – Rhiannon Grant, Anne de Gruchy and Joycelin Dawes – for listening patiently while I thought aloud, and giving me new insights. I am indebted to Joycelin for the concept of the 'inner-side'. My thanks to Gill Pennington and Lee Taylor for generously allowing me to reproduce their 'invited ministry' given at Yearly Meeting 2016, and to Anna Levin for sharing her story. I am grateful also to Marilyn Higgins and Michael Hutchinson for their helpful comments on the text.

INTRODUCTION

When writing this reflection, I had in mind as readers my fellow Friends and those who have heard Quakers talk about a 'concern' and wondered about it. I speak with no authority other than as a member of a Quaker meeting; I do not claim it as any kind of definitive guide, but I hope it will make a contribution to the conversation. It assumes some familiarity with Quaker worship, with the way we conduct our business, and with some of the language we use.

Every experience of concern is unique, but I have tried to discern some general principles, following the course of a concern from the initial promptings, through testing it with our meeting, acting on it, and eventually laying it down. I have also wanted to draw attention to other ways in which we might share our experience of trying to live out our faith in our daily lives.

I have used the first person singular when writing about my personal experience, but 'we' to refer both to our corporate practice and to the experience of individual spiritual leading, to reflect our understanding that it may come to any one of us at any time. I trust that the context makes it clear. I have used lower case to refer to meetings in general, or to the community of the yearly meeting, and capitals to refer to the event of Yearly Meeting or to a specific meeting such as Meeting for Sufferings.

Where I have embedded quotations from *Quaker faith & practice* in the text, I have abbreviated the title of our book of discipline to *Qf&p*. All such quotations come from the current, fifth edition.

CHAPTER 1

How I came to be here

I first came to Friends in 1987. I realised very soon that all my life I had been a Quaker without a meeting – one of those who talk about 'coming home'. One aspect of Quakerism that attracted me strongly was its emphasis on integrity – trying to live our lives always in accordance with what we believe to be true. When I came to Friends, I did not find people who were only 'Sunday Quakers'.

Since then I have continued to learn about this Quaker family of mine and its ways. I have reflected on my personal experience of sharing a leading with my meeting; and as a member of various groups and meetings asked to test a concern. Sometimes it has been an experience of deep, shared discernment, but at other times it has not gone well, and the Friend concerned has felt let down and disappointed – as I did, until I realised that what I had wanted was not what I needed.

I have been in meetings for worship for business where we were asked to consider what seemed to be a 'concern about', an anxiety or reaction to current affairs, a wish that Quakers, or someone, would do something. At other times, it would be clear that the Friend had felt pushed by the Spirit to a course of action, often at some cost to themselves and in spite of difficulties. We had wanted to recognise this sense of a personal leading, but stopped short of uniting with it ourselves. Did either of these situations represent a 'concern', in its distinctive Quaker sense?

In my own case, it was an imperative to act that – although rooted in our peace testimony – seemed to have an indirect relationship to Quaker witness. I felt it nonetheless as a true leading of the Spirit. I started to ask myself questions. What is a concern? What is the dimension that distinguishes it? What about the other words and phrases we use, like 'the promptings of love and truth' or 'leadings'? Do these words denote a different experience? If they are all spiritual, God-given, is it a difference of quality, of degree, of depth? I asked myself if this was just playing with words, or about something fundamentally important to us as Quakers in Britain today. The longer I sat with it, the more questions I asked:

- What does 'acting under concern' feel like? What are the implications?

- What is a meeting doing when it is asked to test a concern?
- Is there a difference between supporting a concern and feeling it laid upon us collectively?
- In today's Quaker culture, how easy is it to speak about or test an inward calling?
- What do Friends expect from their meeting? What do meetings expect of themselves?
- How does this relate to the personal experience of Friends 'pushed by the light'? What do they need from their meeting, and do they receive it?

This was the point at which I applied for an Eva Koch scholarship, realising that I would need some kind of framework to help me make sense of my perplexity. When I heard I had been successful in my application, I greeted the news with a mixture of gratitude and trepidation: now I was committed to trying to answer my questions. As I wrote, some of these questions took different forms, and many more emerged.

This is not a scholarly treatise, or a sociological survey: I do not have the background or gifts for these. I asked to be allowed to explore, and that is what I have done. Explorers do not necessarily have a destination in mind: they follow tracks that look promising, or battle through undergrowth because they see something interesting on the other side. And they observe what they find during their exploration. This is my report on what I have found. I tend to think in images and metaphors and analogies. I will be using some of these because they have helped me towards a clearer understanding. They may resonate with you, or they may not. You will have your own, and you might want to reimagine mine.

Although this reflection is about the meaning and source of concern, inevitably it is about language too, and this is a thread that runs throughout. I ask questions about the language we use, and whether it helps or hinders how we communicate our deepest truths to one another. The fundamentals are already there in our current book of discipline, *Quaker faith & practice*: my starting point and my guide throughout has been chapter 13. I think of this work as a kind of descant on the theme of 'faith in action' (*Qf&p* 13.01–13.18).

I have read, of course, and learnt much. To help me get a picture of Friends' current understanding of concern, I used a questionnaire that I circulated to my area meeting and to other Friends who I felt might have something to say. I am immensely grateful to everyone who took the trouble to complete it, sharing their insights and experience. A workshop run by Michael Hutchinson for South East Scotland Area Meeting in February 2016 moved my thinking on, and helped me to formulate my questions. Ministry in Meeting for Sufferings and at Yearly Meeting has deepened my understanding. So too have many conversations over the past year, as Friends and friends shared their thoughts and insights. Where unattributed, all these various contributions appear as 'Voices' and are set in italics in the text. I have placed them where I consider they best illustrate a point – on a few occasions that has entailed splitting the original contribution between sections.

As I expected, I have found myself changed by this experience: I am more ready to take heed of the promptings of love and truth – in myself and in others.

The words we use and why they matter

"Words are only symbols and when there is no shared experience the symbolism breaks down."

Quaker faith & practice 2.63

Does it matter what language we use? Surely we need to be true to our own experience? Writing in *The Friend*, Craig Barnett of Sheffield & Balby Area Meeting urges us to "...recognise a wide range of experiences, images and symbols as equally important for expressing the full range of Quaker experience." But he also notes that "One of the ways that contemporary Quaker practice has become impoverished is by the loss of a shared spiritual language" (Barnett, 2016, p. 14). In the same piece, he writes that "Quaker practices open us to the possibility of encounter with a reality that may be experienced as personal and impersonal, masculine, feminine, immanent, transcendent or otherwise."

My enquiry into some of the traditional language of Quakerism is not intended to imply that there are prescribed words we should use. As Simon Best, Head of Learning at Woodbrooke, says, "Having a shared spiritual language is not the same as using the same words."[1] The language we use to describe our own spiritual experience points towards something fundamentally unknowable and unsayable. Expressing our sense of this inner life can be difficult: it requires space, time and trust. Listening is a gift we can all offer each other, and when we listen someone into a deeper consideration of their leading, we are hearing their own experience in their own words. But it might help us to have some shared sense of what characterises a leading, or a concern. If we recognise those characteristics, we can use them as our touchstones, regardless of how they are expressed.

Our diffuse use of the word 'concern' goes back a long way: in 1949 Roger Wilson writes, "'Concern' is a word which has tended to become debased by excessively common usage among Friends, so that too often it is used to cover merely a strong desire" (Wilson, 1949, p. 12). We still use it in multiple senses, and we will continue to do so. And as Brenda Heales points out, meanings are never static: "Words change their meanings over the centuries, even over

---

1 Personal communication

the decades" (Heales and Cook, 1992, p. 39). So is there any point in trying to identify a specific Quaker interpretation? This is a question I have asked myself often. But 'bringing a concern to meeting' is an action we can all choose to take. Surely it would help us all if we had a shared understanding of what that means (and does not mean), and shared expectations of the process.

Zélie Gross offers a warning: "A way of using this language worth noting, and perhaps questioning, is when Friends employ Quaker terms to add weight to a point they want to make, or to claim authenticity that puts it beyond challenge. If we spot this way of cloaking ordinary secular impulses, we will need to act tactfully to respond to the real message" (Gross, 2015, p. 291). But as we will see later, some of us might use these Quaker terms because we are not aware of their full implications, or because we are unpractised in sharing our experience in our own words.

I have a sense that we may be inhibiting ourselves unnecessarily. We use the word 'concern' to cover all manner of subjective experience, yet we seem nervous of using other available language to describe more closely our experience of spiritual guidance. If we have only the word 'bird', we cannot make the distinction between a kestrel and a wren, either to ourselves or to others. If we have only 'rain', how would we know whether to prepare for drizzle or a downpour? Our scale of description starts at one end with the small promptings we find it unnecessary to talk about, then leaps, with hardly anything between, to 'having a concern'. It is as if all the marks on a ruler were towards one end, instead of being evenly spaced. We may be in danger of failing to communicate to one another the things that matter in our life as Friends together – perhaps we need to recalibrate that scale. Our language is wonderfully rich and so is our Quaker heritage. Might we try to articulate the distinctive Quaker sense of 'concern' and at the same time find other ways to talk about how we express our faith in action?

CHAPTER 3

Nudgings, promptings, leadings, concerns

"Take heed, dear Friends, to the promptings of love and truth in your hearts. Trust them as the leadings of God whose Light shows us our darkness and brings us to new life."

Advices & queries 1

Of the four words in the chapter title, the first three appeared in the spiritual preparation activities for Yearly Meeting 2016:

- What was it that helped you to be open and to recognise the **nudging** of the Spirit?
- How could you share your **leadings** and understanding?
- Was the **prompting** of the Spirit building on a talent you were already aware of, or by following the prompting did a new gift emerge?

I am going to take it that these are 'words towards' felt and known experiences, not abstractions, and that these are all descriptions of the action of the Spirit on an individual or group. The 2016 Yearly Meeting Epistle acknowledges this in quoting from 1 Corinthians: "There are varieties of gifts, but the same Spirit. There are varieties of service, but the same Lord. There are varieties of activity, but in all of them… the same God is active. In each of us the Spirit is seen to be at work for some useful purpose" (1 Corinthians 12:4–7).

My starting question was "What do we understand by 'concern'?" So for the sake of completeness, I have added it to the list. For reasons that I hope will later become clear, I will begin with it.

What is 'concern'?

The everyday connotations of 'concern' relate to our emotions or interests, but need go no further. There are many things – inequality, the scarcity of bees, unfair trade, UK politics – that make me worried, anxious, 'concerned', sad, passionate, angry even. This kind of concern seems to come with a frown attached. Although I recognise the leadings of others (whether Quaker or not), and I support their work on these issues in small ways, these particular matters are not concerns laid on me as I understand the word when used in a Quaker sense.

First things first. Is it real? Is 'acting under concern' just a quaint, outmoded Quaker phrase, or is it a recognition of a deeper reality, no less authentic for being hard to articulate? The *Oxford English dictionary* helpfully has a section on the Quaker meaning of 'concern': "In the Religious Society of Friends (Quakers): a feeling, arising from an insight into the divine will, that action must be taken on a particular matter. Also in *under concern*: experiencing such a feeling" (OED online).

In the 1883 *Book of Christian Discipline of the Religious Society of Friends in Great Britain* the word 'concern' is not indexed, but it tells us this: "We turn to our dear Friends, both younger and older, who have been led, under the constraining influences of love to Christ, into varied fields of labour amongst those around them. In assuring these of our warm sympathy, we would express the desire that in our various Meetings they may be cheered by the counsel and assistance of Friends…" (p. 62). Here is 'acting under concern' by implication, expressed in language that might be less familiar or comfortable to present-day Friends.

In 1925 'Concerns to be shared' appears in the index: "We are thankful that so often in our common worship, and in our experience of joint responsibility for the service of God's kingdom, as well as in times of private retirement, new impulses are felt towards wider service. It is our earnest hope that Friends will always cherish these impulses, and be willing to share their concerns with others in our meetings, seeking united guidance as to the manner in which the tasks that are laid upon them may be accomplished. It is the privilege of the fellowship to foster the growth of right concerns and to encourage and provide for the development of the service in question. A real concern is a gift from God" (*Christian practice*, 1925). "Counsel", "assistance", "united guidance", "foster", "encourage": it is clear from the language of both these passages that whether or not the word 'concern' is used, sharing our "new impulses" with our meetings is seen as an important, even integral, part of being a member of the Quaker community.

In 1983 Meeting for Sufferings asked Yearly Meeting Agenda Committee to appoint a working party "to consider the nature and variety of concern and the right way of responding to it". The question arose because in the then current *Book of church government* (1968) the word was used both in its specific 'religious concern' sense and in the more general secular sense of issues that worry us. Our current book of discipline, *Quaker faith & practice*, continues to do this. *Advices & queries* 9 advises us, "Yield yourself and all your outward concerns to God's guidance…" while *Advices & queries* 36 asks: "Do you uphold those who are acting under concern, even if their way is not yours?" Chapter 13 gives guidance to Friends about bringing concerns to meeting.

Three years later the working party produced its report. The nine members approached the question under two broad headings, "The Traditional Quaker Religious Concern" and "Matters About Which Friends Become Concerned". The implication is clear: there is a difference. In the introduction the authors quote Samuel Caldwell, General Secretary of Philadelphia Yearly Meeting: "The underlying problem is not verbal, it is theological" (*The nature and variety of concern*, 1986, p. 5). Later they write, "We must emphasise that a strong conviction that God wants something done by someone else, or by Friends generally, or by the Society in an organised way, may be valid prophetic utterance faithfully ministered, but it is not a Quaker concern of the special traditional kind, and therefore requires separate treatment" (ibid., p. 7). This sentence is just as relevant to us today, and shows that we are following a longstanding tradition of confusing ourselves with language. The group does not specify what form this "separate treatment" might take, but I want to return to the idea later.

What is a "Quaker concern of the special traditional kind"? Even this group of experienced, wise Friends could only venture *towards* a definition. But they make certain assumptions: that "the individual believes in a 'personal' God whose purposes can be communicated to her or him directly, through the action of the Holy Spirit" (ibid., p. 6), that it involves voluntary obedience, and that this obedience is an act of faith. They identify the essentials as *commitment* to cooperation with God as a "wise and loving purpose" (ibid., p. 6); belief that one can be *guided*; and sustained *preparedness* to respond. This to me beautifully describes a spiritual leading, but falls short of including a sense of communal support. I believe this is a significant element of concern as we currently understand it. When a concern is brought to a meeting, it is very often in the hope that it will be supported or 'owned': in other words in the belief that this is a call upon Friends more widely. Sometimes the minute recording the meeting's discernment focuses on the content of the concern, or the action to be taken, and pays less attention to the inner spiritual imperative, perhaps taking it as understood.

It seems to me that a Quaker concern has two aspects. It begins when an individual (or group) feels impelled to take action. It may be clear what is required of them, or only that there is something they must do. It is a kind of insistent call that seems both to arise beyond and chime with something deep within. It is persistent: it will not go away. There is a feeling of rightness, which can be hard to explain or define. It is also about content – what is this concern about? The meeting gathers and listens, and it becomes clear that this is central to our identity, an area of witness that defines who we are. There is something in a Quaker concern that is inherently communal: there is a relationship between the individual and the meeting, between personal leading and group discernment. So when we bring a concern to our meeting, it implies two questions: am I rightly led, and am I right to believe that this is something that Friends own collectively? We speak about a 'tested concern' – the point at which the meeting accepts a degree of communal responsibility.

During my time at Woodbrooke, I developed a working definition of what I thought a Quaker concern might be – a kind of compass to guide me. It is the place where our inward calling and the outward expression of Quaker testimony meet. It is where two tributaries converge: the thing that gives cause for concern and the spiritual impulse to act. It invites collective discernment of the rightness of the call and of the course of action we feel it necessary to take. It is a response to circumstances rather than a reaction to events. It arises from our faith and is a manifestation of it.

How do we know?

In *The Q-bit*, Joycelin Dawes writes about the 'inner-side' of trusteeship in relation to Quaker Social Action (Dawes, 2013, p. 6).

The inner-side of concern, the experience, might be described as a leading. This is where it begins.

I have read, and heard, many stories of Friends led to a course of action, who felt in their innermost being that this was something they were called to do. It has come seemingly out of the blue or, perhaps more commonly, where visible injustices or needs demanded a personal response. This was no good idea to be taken up when they had more time, nor a wish that somebody somewhere would do something. It was personal, and it was insistent. There were consequences: obedience to that call did not leave them unchanged, and came at some personal cost.

Many Friends are familiar with Frederick Buechner's description of vocation: "The place God calls you to is the place where your deep gladness and the world's deep hunger meet" (Buechner, 1993, p. 119). 'Vocation' might suggest a lifetime's dedication to a single cause, but the root of the word is 'to call' and we may be called to different service at different times in our lives. Is this a uniquely Quaker experience? Of course not. There are many examples of people of all faiths and none who have what the musician, writer and activist Pat Kane describes as "the burning zeal that perfectly lines up who you are with what you do" (Kane, 2016). A Friend in my area meeting writes, "I believe that in many different religious groups the Spirit still convicts, convinces, places a 'concern'." But there is something distinctively Quaker about how we talk about it, what we believe to be the source, and in our practice of testing – and in our expectation that having recognised a spiritual calling, we as a community of Friends have a responsibility to nurture it and provide support.

It was probably in the 1850s that the term 'inner light' started to be used as a synonym for 'inward light'. I prefer the latter, suggesting as it does something that comes from a place outside the merely human. Many Friends in Britain (at least those who experience the existence of a spiritual reality) are perhaps more comfortable with a God immanent, closer to us than our breath, a resource constantly at hand, on which we draw and from which we can seek guidance. A transcendent God that intervenes, instructs and engages us might be a less comfortable concept. Both are metaphors, pointing towards the unknowable and unsayable.

Nevertheless, much of the language we use takes or implies the passive voice. We are nudged, prompted, led, moved, guided, called. Concerns are laid upon us. Friends may be uncomfortable with the directness of saying "God has spoken to me" – with good reason; but there is a pervading sense, which is supported by personal testimony, of being acted upon. We are asked to respond to a call that has a quality of coming from somewhere other than our own identity, from outside our conscious mind, from a reality that exists outside the boundaries of thought.

This is the first characteristic – a call. It may feel like a change of direction, a specific and unexpected urge to action, or a slow dawning that whatever we have been doing is not enough. There is a sense of rightness, a chiming of the inner and outer, or as when a string is perfectly tuned. This could be because the way ahead is made easier than we had supposed, with unexpected openings and offers of support. Or it may be in spite of obstacles and uncertainty; there is some cost and it often involves personal change, sometimes not explicitly named but present nonetheless.

These characteristics, of inner call and rightness, the effects of change and cost, can help us discern where we are and what we need, for ourselves and for each other. Bringing this leading to a meeting allows us to continue to test it, to ask: 'Am I rightly led?' That's a good enough question in itself, and is worth asking more often than we do. The inner-side must come first. But when we bring a concern to meeting we are asking something more: we are asking Friends to recognise the content of the concern as reflecting something fundamental to our community of Friends – core to our witness in the world. As Joycelin Dawes expresses it, the meeting discerns whether the inward light of the Friend concerned is aligned with the inward light of the community of Friends.[2] It may be a new area of work, or a new application of a concern already supported by Friends. It might be a particular course of action, or, at this stage, a sense that something needs to be done – and done by us.

Here, for me, are the touchstones of concern:

---

2   Personal communication

The individual or group...

- **feels an insistent and persistent sense of being personally called to act.** It may be clear what this action is, or it may only be clear that we must respond to a need in some way.
- **has a sense of inner conviction, and of the rightness of this call.** It may entail internal or external struggles: everything might fall into place easily, or the way can be fraught with difficulty. But the sense of rightness remains.
- **is changed in some way by this experience.** The change may be small or great; it may be gradual or radically different. It might be experienced inwardly and/or be outwardly visible.
- **experiences some personal cost** – however joyfully accepted, in inner or outer resources. The cost might be in terms of time, energy, effort or money expended. Or it might be in risk to respectability, employment or relationships.

The meeting...

- **acknowledges** some or all of these characteristics of a true spiritual leading, and
- **recognises a call to the meeting or to the whole Society of Friends.** It supports the concern as an expression of our faith in practice undertaken by, with and for Friends.

We talk about 'holding a concern'. I like this image: it suggests something about steadfastness, about it being more than an individual, about Friends feeling held by and within the group. This is where I wish I could draw. I have a vivid picture of an umbrella of concern, held by the local, area or yearly meeting, sheltering Friends acting under it.

What if it is not a concern?

This depiction of a concern sets the bar quite high. Is it all or nothing? Either a 'traditional Quaker concern' or an experience of no value?

Not at all. We have those other very helpful concepts at our disposal: nudgings, promptings and leadings. They are all expressions of the Spirit at work.

Imagine a packet of cress seeds. Imagine some damp kitchen towel. The cress will grow, as much as it can, and for as long as it can. And then it will stop growing. That is the image that comes to me when I think about my daily life. I write a letter in support of a cause, or sign a petition. I am prompted to do so by a need there in front of me. It may be a temporary, passing issue, but I believe it to have good and worthwhile aims, and it is a small way in which I can put my faith into practice. I might feel nudged into visiting a neighbour or making a phone call to let someone know that I care; or feel unexpectedly that I need to uphold someone in prayer. A prompting like this may come to an individual and quickly spread through the meeting – for example, a spontaneous vigil at the site of a violent incident. But in general we do not need to take it to our meeting because it makes no great demands on us, costs us nothing significant, involves no change in us, and we do not see it as a new expression of our communal life as Quakers.

Now imagine an oak tree, broad and strong, its roots reaching deep and wide as its crown. The acorn took a while to germinate, but even before that, interesting and invisible things were happening inside it. Once it germinated, it needed nourishing soil and protection from being trampled. Now it has a strength and a life of its own. Here is our corporate tested concern, rooted in and growing out of Quaker beliefs. It illustrates the way that "our faith seeks to implement timeless values in a world of change" (Dale, 1996, p. 50).

What about a leading – supposing that is the experience of many of us, from time to time? A sense that there is something we must do, a spiritual imperative to take a course of action. It might seem like an accumulation of small but insistent promptings. We may feel we are asked to use our gifts more fully; or to do more than react, and to respond more deeply to a situation or a need. It includes something about commitment.

We might be pushing the botanical metaphor too far now, but perhaps this is the herbaceous border: tall and short plants, spiky and smooth-leaved, the longer-lasting and the more ephemeral. A multiplicity of shape and form, blooming at different times, making a harmonious but varied whole. It seems to me that much of the life of witness of our meetings might lie here as we follow the leadings of the Spirit. Planting the stately oak tree of a tested concern of the yearly meeting is a rarer event. Equally, our promptings and leadings might be the leaves on that tree. Each leaf converts the light that it receives into nourishment – without them, the tree will die. The life and witness of individual Friends and their meetings give life in turn to our corporately held concerns and testimonies, which would otherwise be empty words.

What we might call a leading will have the characteristics of calling and rightness, and perhaps the effects of change and cost. It may relate to a concern already held by the wider Society. It might be work in the world that arises from our testimony – to simplicity, or peace, or equality – but does not need endorsement from the meeting as a whole. Perhaps Quakers as a body have no particular expertise or history in this area; perhaps its strongest connection is with a non-Quaker organisation; or the work does not require us to identify ourselves as Quakers. We might still want to share and test this leading with our meeting, but stop short of bringing it as a concern.

None of these – nudgings, promptings, leadings, concerns – are more, or less, important and valuable. They are different but they each have the same source. They are all manifestations of our faith in practice. Nor are they set in opposition to each other: they are on a continuum. A concern may not – probably does not – start with a blinding flash of insight. Its origins may lie in a growing sense of an impulse to act, felt by a single person or by several individuals separated by time or distance. At some point Friends might come to understand that they are called to own this concern as communally theirs. This will not necessarily be a speedy process, and we need to be patient with ourselves and each other, however pressing it feels. Jenny Routledge writes about her concern for revitalising eldership: "The process took two years of formal and informal testing, threshing meetings, workshops, business meetings, reports, articles in the newsletter, [and] talking to Friends… Throughout this long and difficult time I kept going, I was upheld, loved and had a sense that I was being Spirit-led" (Routledge, 2014, pp. 10–11).

Corporate recognition by the yearly meeting can take months, sometimes even years or generations. Meanwhile the concern is held by individuals, supported by their meetings. It took a long time before Britain Yearly Meeting was able to unite in support of same-sex marriage, but for many years individuals and meetings expressed their leadings that "marriage… is the Lord's work" (*Qf&p* 16.01) in a variety of ways, including celebrations of commitment.

CHAPTER 4

Being led

"Others have spoken of a moment of calling, of an overwhelming sense of love and light, leading to a certainty that they must act… the message came opposite to the war memorial: '*You* shall do it and *I* shall help'. This message was the driving force."
George Murphy, from *Quaker faith & practice* 13.04

It begins with personal experience, because this is not about an abstraction: it is human beings who hear the call.

A leading might begin with an unexpected jolt, or an accumulation of these small promptings; a sudden realisation or a slow dawning over weeks and months. We begin to feel called to a course of action rather than to a single act. We may be excited, daunted, or unsure where we are being taken.

Beth Allen reminds us that "Sometimes, instead of feeling the push inwardly, in our own hearts, the leading comes through another person suggesting something to us or asking us to do something, but we need to confirm this outward leading by looking for an inward answering. Often, Friends ask us to take on a routine job which just keeps our little bit of the Quaker world functioning… This too can be a leading" (Allen, 2007, p. 37).

The language used in these quotations is varied, and sometimes 'concern' is used where we might prefer 'leading': the inner-side of a concern. There is no hard and fast division. A leading could be an emerging concern: the Friend who is led may in time become 'the Friend concerned', as the sense grows that this is a call on, and to, the Society. Michael Birkel quotes Rufus Jones: "The best proof that the seed which one plants is an acorn is that it grows into an oak" (Birkel, 2013, p. 254).

Human language is inadequate to describe the source of our leadings, but we do have access to descriptions of how it feels. The following words express something of the experience of being led.

VOICES

A call

"A divine imperative to action laid inwardly upon a person…"
(*The nature and variety of concern*, 1986, p. 13)

"The true 'concern' [emerges as] a gift from God, a leading of his spirit which may not be denied… The individual… knows, as a matter of inward experience, that there is something that the Lord would have done, however obscure the way, however uncertain the means to human observation." (Wilson, 1949, p. 12)

Something extraneous to oneself… a revelation. [It comes]
from God; from deep in us; from the heart; light; energy;
passion; absolute imperative. [Responses from a workshop]

It's coming through [not from] me.
It comes from outside me, but is contiguous with my being.
I more often use the word 'calling', rather than leading, it feels
more like that physically – or more like a kick up the butt!
I sure wish I was being led, but I feel like I'm being pushed.

A sense of being reluctantly led to undertake a task.

A true note

On a very few occasions I have felt that I have been led in
a totally unexpected direction towards something that felt
absolutely right.
It gave me a strong conviction that this is what I had to do
and a calm certainty.

The sense of rightness came only after I fully committed to
following the call.

It doesn't feel like having a choice.

You know what it is when it happens.
Everything's aligned, like riding a motorbike through bends.
A sense of spiritual liberation.

These personal accounts can point to something interesting: that we may not be fully aware at the time of what is happening. We might see where the story began only when we are a few chapters further on.

Barry and Jill Wilsher, in a letter describing the origins of the Quaker Peace Action Caravan, say, "There was from the early stages of our discussion together a strong sense of the 'rightness' of what we were talking about. The ideas flowed freely, and although we were not conscious of it at the time, we would say now that we were clearly working under guidance" (*Qf&p* 13.03). "Its roots go back further by a couple of years than we have actually described, but we would be surprised if this did not prove to be a common factor in all work undertaken under concern" (*The nature and variety of concern*, 1986, p. 22).

In face-to-face conversations, something else stood out that could not be seen in the written responses. When I asked where they felt that sense of rightness, and very often even when I did not, Friends gestured to the centre of their body – never to their head, and never to somewhere 'out there'.

Change

"They were changed men themselves before they went about to change others."

William Penn, from Quaker faith & practice 19.48

"Neither of us could be thought of as 'peace activists'."

The nature and variety of concern, 1986, p. 21

I felt I was in touch with something that was needed, that was
shared in some ways with others, like a common river flowing,
but was harder to see than that.
It gave me new perspectives.

I had been well known in the meeting... as a person who was not a great enthusiast for 'witness'.

I find I can do things I thought I couldn't.
It gave me great courage... I later did not feel fearful even in very testing situations.
I had to speak my truth in a way I'd never had to before –
I never thought I could have done that.
I almost lose the ego bit of who I am.

[After the death of my partner in concern] I still feel I hold the concern: change continues – there is an extra inflowing of the spirit.
It changed my relationship with my meeting.
My sense of myself as a disability activist in wider society.

Cost

By 'cost' I do not mean to imply hair shirts or grudging sacrifice – only that if we are serious about heeding the call, it does require something of us. Inner and outer resources are drawn on, at different times. Our life may be affected in ways we had not anticipated.

"For this I can say, I... joyfully entered prisons as palaces, telling mine enemies to hold me there as long as they could: and in the prisonhouse I sung praises to my God, and esteemed the bolts and locks put upon me as jewels..."
William Dewsbury, from *Quaker faith & practice* 19.33

"We have heard that five Friends who participated at the No Faith in Trident day of action at Burghfield on Monday 27th June 2016 are expected to appear in court."
MfS/16/07/06 Court and prison register

It led me to move from financial security to insecurity.

*It made me more committed to something that could actually go
against my best interests and wellbeing!
It is utterly terrifying when I think about it: the vulnerability of
being at the mercy of an inexorable force like an earthquake.
Only once in my life have I acted under concern. No choice,
unnerving, frightening.*

*I found it challenging – as I know others did – to stand up
and give a personal statement in public outside the safety of a
Quaker context.*

*The mystery of it became a burden because I knew all I had to
do was to wait in the light, but that didn't seem enough... I still
ask, what should I be doing? And I don't know the answer.*

Disappointment, even grief, as others fall away.

The cost can be in seemingly mundane matters – but time, energy,
effort and enthusiasm are valuable resources.

*He hired the hall, did some local advertising, designed some
posters and organised their printing.*

CHAPTER 5

Sitting with it

"Achieving clarity about a concern is a particular exercise in discernment. It is a process that begins with considerable private reflection and the asking of some tough questions. Is this a desire that someone else do something or is it really a call to act oneself? Is this concern in keeping with the testimonies of the Society? Is it genuinely from God?"

Quaker faith & practice 13.05

It is evident by now that the process of testing starts with us as individuals, as soon as we ask ourselves questions. We stand in the light – the light that discovers, uncovers. It is an interior examination of the heart and soul, a checking-in with God. Ben Pink Dandelion offers a model (courtesy of Stan Thornburg) of the testing process for discerning whether it is right to offer spoken ministry in meeting for worship (Pink Dandelion, 2007, p. 215). We might want to follow a similar process, returning always to the centre.

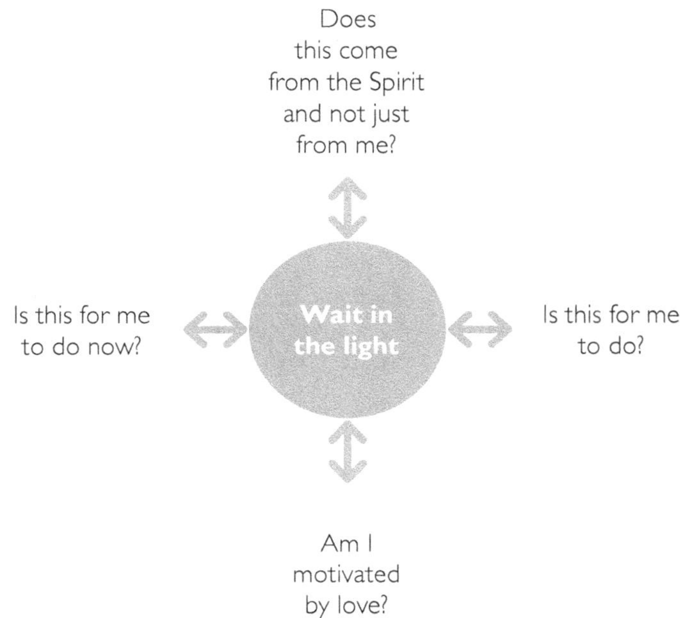

Other questions will follow. How does this sit with our current expressions of testimony? What inner and outer resources do I have to contribute? Do I have enough knowledge or experience of the situation or need? Do I need to learn more? Who can help me? What practical assistance might I need?

Even when thoroughly immersed in the task we have been given, we will need to step back from time to time and reflect. Do I still hear that call? Is this still for me to do? Am I still motivated by love, pushed by the light? Testing, whether it is personal or communal, is not a single event in time.

We may not feel yet that we need to bring this sense of a leading to the meeting formally, but want to share with one or two trusted Friends. Trusted to listen, but also trusted to challenge us in love. They might see a pattern, or a change in us: it is not easy to be both the observer and the observed, and they could see something we do not. A first step might be to talk to an elder or overseer, or we might want a small group to help us by holding a meeting for clearness. There is a useful leaflet produced by Quaker Life called *Clearness*, which sets out why and how we might do this.[3]

At this point the question might simply be "Please will you help me discern whether I am rightly led?". Or as the working party puts it: "I am reporting to [my] Meeting what I believe God has laid on me: please can we search together in prayer and worship to see whether this is actually what God wants?" (*The nature and variety of concern*, 1986, p. 8). This language may be difficult for us as Friends nowadays, with our different understandings of the will of God. Nonetheless I think this is pointing to something important: that testing a concern or leading must first involve listening to the inner experience. However expressed, whether in the traditional language used in 1986, or in more hesitant words expressing an urge, a drive, an insistence coming from outside one's usual self and as a deep sense of rightness, it lies in the souls that have heard a call.

---

3 Available online at www.quaker.org.uk/documents/clearness-meeting-guidance-2012

Voices

*Over a period of months a disquiet… grew until it became
a 'concern' placed upon me and which I felt compelled to
respond to.*

*I felt an extraordinary clarity and joy in the midst of uncertainty:
I felt I was walking an unknown path in the dark, but someone
was holding my hand.*

It allowed me to become clearer.

*I'm learning obedience to a call, no matter what it might mean
to my life.*

*[I took it] not to the meeting per se, but to some wise Friends
who listened and encouraged me to follow the leading of the
spirit. I had no expectations other than non-judgemental
listening… non-judgemental listening was what I got.*

This is an age where the individual is paramount. We prize diversity
of spiritual experience and its expression. It is not easy to come with
humility and trust to the guidance of the Spirit and the collective
wisdom of the group in channelling that guidance. Finding the
words for something that lies beyond words is hard too. It is a process
that needs mutual trust. From the meeting, it requires open hearts,
tender listening and thoughtful discernment.

CHAPTER 6

Taking it further

"The discernment process is not confined to solitary reflection. As a Religious Society we are more than a collection of people who meet together – we meet as we do because we believe that gathered together we are capable of greater clarity of vision. … This is both a further part of the testing process and an expression of our membership in a spiritual community. It is a recognition of mutual obligations: that of a Friend to test the concern against the counsel of the group and that of the group to exercise its judgment and to seek the guidance of God."

Quaker faith & practice 13.05

So far, we have been exploring the foothills of concern – the sense of being called to action. What next?

Margaret Heathfield sets out the importance of seeking corporate discernment. "Any judgement made from our own perspective is bound to be insufficient as the ultimate test. This is why in matters of great moment, when promptings were sufficiently powerful to threaten the taking over of the major part of one's life, and began to merge into that other, larger concept of 'concern', Friends have valued the spiritual community of the Meeting. Here, the individual was known and understood, but the great principles of Truth were valued just as much as the individual Friend. Thus the prompting might be seen more clearly, in a wider, truer perspective" (Heathfield, 1994, pp. 36–37).

Sometimes our local meeting is not the right place to start: it might be more helpful to become involved with one of the Quaker recognised bodies[4] as a way of deepening our understanding and linking with Friends under the same concern. Margaret Heathfield again: "The practice of testing our promptings and our concerns with our local group does not always hold good, and when Friends find a lack of sympathy or spiritual fellowship within their local meeting, they look outside the Quaker circle to find support, or they find other Friends from further afield who share their interest. This wandering to find soul-mates has encouraged a fascinating range of

---

4   These used to be known as listed informal groups: "independent groups through which Friends may share common interest, seek affirmation or carry out witness" (*Qf&p* 13.19).

Special Interest Groups to be set up, as well as much ecumenical and other joint activity" (Heathfield, 1994, pp. 68–69).

What are we asking?

A quick glance through any thesaurus will give us tens of synonyms and hundreds of related words for 'testing'. What does testing mean in the context of our Quaker practice? What does it not mean? Whatever it is, it is a process that we do *with* each other, not *to* each other, and it is a continuation of the inner testing already begun. It is not about whether we are good enough or spiritual enough, and it is not about being judged. Nor is it bringing a good idea or asking for backing for a particular course of action. The working party "found it necessary to spell out what 'I am asking you to test my concern' does and does not mean. It does *not* mean, for example, 'I think I should do this, and I'd like to know if you agree with me, Friends'. Nor does it mean 'Would Friends agree that Quaker funds should be made available to make possible what I am suggesting?'" (*The nature and variety of concern*, 1986, p. 8).

What have we done so far? We have tested our leading within ourselves and with a few Friends or with our local meeting. We have said, 'This I feel called to do', or 'I must do what I can, although I am not yet clear what that is'. They have helped us to disentangle the personal issues and emotions, and have strengthened our sense that we are led to do this work. And perhaps that is all that is needed: the love, support and interest of our own local meeting. By 'letting it in on the ground floor' we have involved our meeting in the story as it unfolds.

The meeting may recognise our concern as having a specifically local context, answering a need that has arisen in our town or village. We might want to let other Friends know about it through a report in the area meeting newsletter, for example, and that might be a way to make useful connections.

"Some concerns can be expressed, fully tested and then supported within the local meeting."

The nature and variety of concern, 1986, p. 9

> **A story of a local concern:** Quaker Week 2015 was fast approaching:
> a sudden flash of inspiration – a bright idea – a leading – came to me.
> Why not do something in the neighbouring town, where there had been
> no meeting for over 100 years? It felt like time to be more adventurous.
> Friends supported the idea and began to plan. One of the main moving
> forces was a new attender. He was really keen as he wanted to find
> out more about Quakers for his own benefit. He booked the town
> hall, designed some posters and organised their printing. The more
> experienced amongst us provided the substance, planning sessions on
> why we were Quakers and then on the testimonies. More than 20
> people came to the first session and there was surprising enthusiasm
> for a regular series of meetings. We followed specific requests from the
> people who came, for example, to talk about the peace testimony. The
> periods of silent worship gradually grew longer. Our embryonic planning
> group began to meet regularly, and we drew on expertise within our
> meeting to enrich the input to our sessions. We have people from
> neighbouring meetings and from other churches, and a few unattached
> seekers. Sometimes we have felt a bit directionless, but [a year later]
> it's still going. It has been taxing for me personally in a number of ways,
> but it has subtly invigorated our meeting, not so much with new people
> attending, but in breathing new life into those already there.

Perhaps the concern is already held by Friends corporately, and our
leading is to play a more active, or different, part in furthering that
concern. Like the oak leaf, we are converting the light that is given
to us into nourishment for the whole tree. For example, in response
to current events, we may feel personally called to play a more active
part in opposing the arms trade. Our meeting may in turn feel led
to do more – hold a collection for Campaign Against Arms Trade;
write to politicians; invite them to a meeting; book a coach to join
with a vigil at an arms fair; stage its own vigil at the gates of a local
business connected to the arms trade; pay our train fare; arrange to
feed the cat if we are arrested – any, some or all of these. Afterwards

we could share our experience with other meetings by submitting it to the Quakers in Britain website at www.quaker.org.uk/our-work/our-stories.

At some point we, and our local meeting, might begin to feel as though something more is required, and we want to take it to the area meeting for further discernment. It takes trust, and often courage, but it can be helpful to be heard by Friends who do not know us so well. It is worth bearing in mind that there is no hierarchy here. Our area meeting is the place where the Venn diagram of local meetings intersects, made up of people just like us. The Friends present may not bring any more 'weightiness' or wisdom, but they do bring a fresh perspective, and a willingness to listen and discern. "The vital thing is that the concern be real and be thoroughly tested" (Dale, 1996, p. 97). One respondent to my questionnaire felt that the practice of testing "helps support people's mental health, as it tests some sense of calling, of living with that which is beyond us as individuals."

It will help everyone if we are clear what we are asking the area meeting; and clear that we have done everything we can as individuals and as a local meeting.

- We may need wider discernment of the rightness of the leading. This need might be felt by our local meeting, if it lacks the necessary experience; or if it is very small, so that it is hard not to be influenced by personal relationships.
- We may feel clear about our leading, but less clear about the action we need to take.
- We may be asking for spiritual and practical support – some sense of ownership – believing that this is an area of work that resonates with our expressions of testimony.
- We might need legal expertise, or the authority of the area meeting to approach other bodies.
- Our concern could benefit from the wider connections of the area meeting and beyond – ecumenical and interfaith, parliamentary work, activist or interest groups, local charities.
- Our local meeting might feel that it is right to release us from other Quaker service, or to seek some financial support from the area meeting.

- We may have reached a point when we simply want to share our sense of excitement or trepidation (or both) as we try to respond to this call.

So we talk, or write, to the clerk of the area meeting, or our local meeting sends a minute.

"The ground of our work lies in our waiting on and listening for the Spirit. Let the loving spirit of a loving God call us and lead us. These leadings are both personal and corporate. If they are truly tested in a gathered meeting we shall find that the strength and the courage for obedience are given to us."

Quaker faith & practice 29.02

VOICES

The relationship between the individual and the meeting

I would like to emphasise how crucial the support of the meeting is to the testing and development of an individual's or group's concerns.
It couldn't have happened if our meeting(s) hadn't been so supportive.
If we listen to the spirit in meeting for worship, and if we test concerns through discernment, we may have fewer concerns, but be more effective.

Quaker gifts include plain speaking. It may lift you up and put you down somewhere else.

What is your personal experience of bringing a concern to meeting?

I became aware of a different quality of listening.
Truth sweeping through the room.
It wouldn't be 'me' asking: it would be the leading and Friends would be being asked to follow a leading, not me.

*You need to be clear about what exactly the concern is about.
Is it actually about your inner call to take more risk, to live out
your faith?
I needed to be careful it wasn't just my need to be useful. But
actually, why not? Maybe it's a divine nudging to use my gifts
for good.*

*I felt led rather unwillingly to speak about my concern. I did
not know what to expect and was very apprehensive and even
reluctant to bring the concern to my LM [but] the way I was
listened to and supported enabled me to find the strength to take
the concern to AM and then to our Sufferings representatives.
It changed the way I understood BYM as an organisation,
Quaker business method, right ordering, personal discernment
and group clearness process as well as the testimony to equality.*

*What I realised, and have further discerned since, was that there
were two very separate things: one is the subject of my calling,
which is mighty complicated stuff; the other, quite separate, is
the nature and process of a concern in a Quaker meeting.*

What are the challenges?

*Concern has the potential to challenge – it can be divisive.
It can have sharp edges.
It can sometimes be a bruising experience. If it seems to be
rejected, it may be being extended and clarified.
It's about stepping with uncertainty.
Friends have been supportive but haven't taken it on. I can't
expect my concern to be the concern of Friends if I haven't been
prepared to be vulnerable.*

*I felt very inadequately prepared for the area meeting, as no one
had walked this route from [my meeting] before.
I think part of the 'problem', for want of a better word… is the lack
of familiarity with some Quaker processes. When this started, [my
small meeting] didn't even have business meetings, so there was no*

'channel' for group discernment or even for taking things from our meeting to area meeting – and beyond. We did have a meeting for clearness, but even then, the four of us present had very different expectations of what a meeting for clearness actually was.

The group can offer very valuable wisdom and discipline but they can also be wrong… an eccentric or unusual person's creative concern could be stifled by a group.

I know people… who were very unclear and unsatisfied by the process. I think they thought it was about getting 'backing' and so were in some ways let down, and they felt like an outsider.

What do you understand by 'testing a concern'?

Whether and in what way the Spirit… is happening.
For working out as to whether this was a discerned concern, or just some academic… niche thinking.

The Friend concerned was able to articulate doubts and certainties and the members of the group asked a lot of penetrating, searching questions, which enabled the Friend to clarify the way forward and also be able to 'take the meeting along', which would certainly not have happened easily without the testing.

On reading Chapter 13 I am struck by the huge responsibility the meeting or group has when a concern is brought before them. We could devote an entire meeting for worship to testing a concern.

Our aim is to establish the kingdom of heaven on earth. The pressure of the world may lead us to feel we have to be hasty. Together we can achieve so much more.
Unless we can do things in love they're not worth doing.
Testing may test all of us and our commitment: it was we who were being tested.

We were being asked to listen to God's voice coming through this Friend.

It may be a long and arduous journey. We asked ourselves: Why are we doing this? We went back to basics – this is why we're doing it.

What are the meeting's responsibilities?

"A concern that is brought before a meeting should be considered with the greatest love, kindness and discipline. Much as we like to support our Friends in the things for which they have an unbounded enthusiasm, it is no kindness to recognise as a concern something which has not received the fullest attention possible."

Quaker faith & practice 13.09

Continual corporate discernment – not a one-off event. It's the start of a process of seeking truth together.
It may tick all the boxes, but it's the way it's carried forward that matters.

The meeting took seriously the spiritual nature of the concern – this was not just 'another discussion topic' but was treated with respect.
The concern that had been raised by another meeting was read out after a meeting for worship for our response. After some space and thought we discussed how to respond. As a series of study evenings had been suggested we agreed to adopt the concern as the topic and explore this more deeply… we took it up and applied ourselves thoroughly.

So – what are you going to do?

I'd support this in some way, I recognise it, but I don't feel it's laid on me to do more.

What can help us?

A clearer understanding of unofficial Quaker 'hierarchy'.

Some framing of the testing by the clerk.

Minutes of meetings often focus on the outward expression of a concern. They use administrative words like 'accept', 'endorse' or 'support' to describe what the meeting has decided. Those kinds of words are necessary, but if that is all that is recorded, I think it is a pity. It may reflect the difficulty of expressing the inexpressible, but it could also reflect discomfort with the deep, loving, sometimes painful listening that is needed. If we do not open ourselves to listen, we will not hear the language of leadings. We will have missed the vital spark. "To give account of how God is shaping our lives and to record our leadings and the working out of testimony today, we must record not only what we do but why and how we have come to do that particular thing" (Davis, 2008, p. 41). Like Christine Davis, I want our minutes to refer to the inner-side, the foundation of any concern. Our touchstones are a sense of being called and of rightness; and the effects are change and cost. None of these terms is used in this extract from a letter from a local meeting, but we hear them, beneath the words:

> "Her journey through this time has moved from a personal difficulty to a political outrage to a Quaker sense of spiritual concern: that she is being tasked to use her skills as a writer, editor and journalist to let these stories be heard, to raise wider awareness of this unreported issue and to keep asking the deeper unanswered questions involved. We would like to bring this concern to Area Meeting, seeking to bring greater discernment to this complex issue."

"At each stage Friends will try to bring their insights to bear. Be prepared for their comments to cause some soul-searching and possible revisions" (*Qf&p* 13.08). It may not be a smooth sequence of steps, and we need to be ready for that. Perhaps the meeting

> **This story could be described as a meeting recognising a leading, but not (yet) adopting a concern:** The Friends who know her best (i.e. in her local meeting) are clear that she has felt truly led by something more than a personal interest. It involves research into complex scientific issues, about which most people, including Friends, are ill-informed. The area meeting minutes its acknowledgement of this leading and offers encouragement and a support group. It stops short of uniting with it yet as a concern: it is not clear what the outcome of the research will be and there is not yet a course of action for the meeting to take. At this point there is no need or reason to extend the discernment to a wider body of Friends.

feels able to give us the support we ask for, or we come away with encouragement to do some more thinking and personal discernment before returning to the meeting. We should not feel disheartened: this can be a necessary process that provides a firmer foundation to build on. The meeting may feel, at least at this stage, that the action does not sit as a core part of 'who we are', but if they have recognised it as a true leading, Friends will still want to give support. Asking us what we need might be a helpful question. Jenny Routledge writes about her experience of bringing her concern to her meeting: "I can see now that although my local meeting and my area meeting were at one with the transformative experience that had led me to a concern, they were not clear what I wanted to do. And I wasn't clear either" (Routledge, 2014, p. 9).

If alternatives to the proposed action are suggested, it should be done with sensitivity, recognising the time and thought already expended. Where the meeting is unable to reach unity, or there is disagreement about the right course of action, a specially convened threshing meeting can help to move the meeting on,[5] providing a safe space to air different perspectives.

---

5 Available online at www.quaker.org.uk/documents/threshing-meeting-guidance-2011.pdf

"It may be determined that the concern is not in harmony with the testimonies of our Society. It should be remembered, however, that:

> 'It is with individuals rather than with communities that new truth originates… While corporate guidance is of great value in controlling individual extravagance, it is a source of great danger to the church if it is opposed to a genuine individual concern.'
> William Charles Braithwaite, 1909

Both individual and meeting should pay heed to the advice: 'Think it possible that you may be mistaken'."

Quaker faith & practice 13.10

Letting go

We might have surprisingly mixed feelings when our concern is recognised and adopted by the meeting. On the one hand, we are glad to have this acknowledgement, which after all is what we sought. On the other, our concern now 'belongs' to a wider group. We are sharing something deeply personal to us, which may by now be a significant part of our life. We will have put energy, time and effort into learning about the issue. It could be disconcerting to find that the meeting has other ideas. It might feel particularly difficult when the meeting unites with the underlying concern, but offers alternatives to our carefully thought-out plan of action. For the work to progress, it will be important to be able to let go to some extent. A Friend comments, "It's amazing what can be achieved when you don't care who achieves it." We need to allow others to be involved, and accept help gratefully.

As Christine Davis says, "The concern takes on a life which is broader than the thoughts of the initiator: it feeds the originator as much as it is fed by that individual. We do not own our concerns; we are stewards of them. We take care of the work, and the work influences who we are" (Davis, 2008, p. 50).

Friends have told me that the meeting's recognition of the concern helped to nourish their own sense that they were rightly guided and gave them strength to overcome obstacles and times of self-doubt. Inevitably there will be setbacks and times of tiredness, but the sense of rightness remains. Christine Davis again, writing about the work of Peace House and of the Scottish Centre for Nonviolence: "There were times when they were tired and dispirited, but the spark of the tested concern was always there" (Davis, 2008, p. 85).

As we continue to test our sense of calling with ourselves and with others, we may find that the underlying concern remains, while the expression of it in outward action varies, as it should, in response to changing circumstances and needs.

Laying down

It might seem strange to talk at this point about laying down a concern, but it is an integral part of the arc of discernment undertaken by the meeting and the Friend in question. A concern that takes the form of a specific action may have a natural life-cycle. Perhaps it is a programme or project to meet a need which no longer exists, or which is now being met in other ways. We may become aware that we have done all we can and may no longer have that sense that it is laid upon us to do. It would be a mistake to continue out of a sense of duty, or out of a sense that other Friends expect it of us. Naturally if the fundamental need is still there, we hope that there will be others who 'catch fire' and can continue the work. Some wise succession planning, harnessing new energy and new leadings, can help to ensure the work goes on even when for us personally the time has come to lessen our involvement.

There should be the same care and thoughtful discernment at the laying down of a concern as there was at its beginning. It is a time to record achievement and give thanks:

"When a concern has run its course, consideration should be given to how this may be recognised and acknowledged. A meeting that has supported a concern should be informed when it is seen to be right to lay that concern down. Celebration for the right ending of what was rightly begun may be appropriate."

Quaker faith & practice 13.13

Candle or conflagration?

"Do you uphold those who are acting under concern, even if their way is not yours?"

Advices & queries 36

In a report on area meeting responses to Meeting for Sufferings, "one Friend said that, although the AM had tested concerns, they were being actively pursued by only a small number of Friends."

I imagine that anyone who feels that compelling urge to action cannot understand why others have not 'caught fire' too: I have made that mistake myself. But fire is hottest at its centre, and cooler towards the edges. It would be a rare meeting where every single member hears the same call and feels the same passion. That does not mean they do not recognise it, but only a few may feel led to commit to practical help. The respondent who said, "I can't expect my concern to be the concern of Friends" might have meant, "I can't expect my personal leading to be experienced by all Friends." To the query at the head of this chapter I would add, 'even if you do not feel the same inward call'.

'Acknowledge', 'support', 'adopt', 'endorse', 'unite with', 'uphold', 'approve', 'accept', 'agree'. However it is expressed in the minute, the meeting has in some way accepted our request to hold the concern. It touches on ownership, or perhaps stewardship. With stewardship comes responsibility. Having made this decision, there is a responsibility on the meeting to do what it can to further it. The meeting is the soil in which the concern is rooted. What nutrients can it provide? However many or few are actively engaged, there is an obligation on all of us, whatever else we do, to prayerfully uphold those acting under concern. It is a tested, supported concern of the meeting: we have said so.

"Meetings that support a Friend's concern will sometimes assume the financial responsibility for the concern. Whether or not this is so, they may also consider offering other forms of help…" (*Qf&p* 13.13). Corporate support could take many forms, and different forms at different times. The meeting might appoint a small support group, or provide practical help in whatever ways are appropriate, linking Friends with expertise and experience, making those wider connections beyond the meeting. It needs to remember too that it is not the only community involved: there is likely to be an impact, direct or indirect, on the family and close friends of the Friend under concern, and this can lead to tensions.

VOICES

All my experience is in large meetings where it has been possible to accept the concern as a matter for the meeting but then to have a smaller number of individuals carrying the concern forward.

I get support when I ask for it (press conferences, meetings, demos).

There must be a difference between a meeting fostering a concern (supporting the person with the concern) and a meeting 'adopting' a concern as its own. I imagine that 'being laid upon us collectively' would spark in everyone this burning need to follow the call.

If I was suddenly led into a challenging development of the concern, which affected members of the meeting directly, it might be 'interesting' and I might well feel at times that I expect too much.

I was 'the Friend concerned' and I was very aware that I was engaging with the concern on behalf of many others whose support and involvement was increasingly encouraged through our work together.

Sometimes concerns are forwarded to another meeting. I moved house two years ago. I arranged for my post to be forwarded, the expectation being that it would not be opened. It does sometimes happen that a concern is forwarded in just such a way – without being opened to consideration, and without the members of the meeting allowing themselves to be opened. This is of no service to anyone.

It is a different matter if the meeting has done all it can, or needs something more than it can provide – and the minute would reflect that.

CHAPTER 8

Widening the orbit

"One part of the discernment process is judging at what point a concern has been considered by all appropriate bodies."

Quaker faith & practice 13.06

How and when does a concern become corporately held by Friends in Britain?

"We… raised the possibility of recognition by Meeting for Sufferings. He [Stephen Thorne, then Recording Clerk] pointed out that would give Meeting for Sufferings the right to appoint to our group, which was clearly inappropriate at that stage. We had already decided some time before *not* to add to our numbers, as we were well tuned-in to working together, so fresh members would have to learn what we had learned all over again. It was a purely personal concern accepted by us all as something laid upon us to do – and we just carried on!"

Anna Bidder, in a letter about the origin of the group that produced *Towards a Quaker View of Sex* (*The nature and variety of concern*, 1986, p. 23)

Sometimes the area meeting considers that the concern should rightly be held by the wider body of Friends across the yearly meeting. A minute might be sent to Meeting for Sufferings. This should not be seen as passing on responsibility, and the meeting will continue to hold the concern and actively support the Friend(s) involved.

Brenda Heales and Chris Cook identify a personal leading becoming a 'public concern' as the point at which it is brought to Meeting for Sufferings (*Seeds of the Spirit*, 2004). By this expression they do not necessarily mean a statement to the outside world, only that the yearly meeting supports the concern. They are writing about Appleseed, a concern that gave Friends new ways to be with God and express that response in images – of the heart and soul rather than the head.

It may take a roundabout route: Quaker author Jim Pym writes that "the concern [acceptance of spiritual healing as a valid part of Quaker history and testimony] actually arose at the committee meeting of the Friends Fellowship of Healing. We accepted it at this time, and it was taken and 'tested' by some members at their area meetings, then brought back and submitted to Sufferings."[6]

VOICES

The concern was adopted and resulted in the work of the Friends involved spreading to meetings across the country.

I became clearer as together we moved through the different stages of reflecting in local meeting and [area] meeting, nominating a… working group, liaising with Friends House staff and preparing written material for Sufferings.

These public or corporate concerns are discerned by Friends as being core expressions of our faith. In procedural terms this might happen when an area meeting has offered it to Meeting for Sufferings for further discernment. Just as area meetings are where local meetings intersect, Meeting for Sufferings, between annual Yearly Meetings, is the place where voices from all of our area meetings can be heard. Discernment is widened and insights can be shared. It is fed by the Spirit at work across the yearly meeting, so that there might be several related minutes of concern coming to it at the same time.

Two of the functions of Meeting for Sufferings are:

- "to deliberate on how best to support the spiritual life of the yearly meeting and to further the development of its visionary and prophetic role;
- to keep under review and to test as appropriate the existing and new concerns referred to it by area meetings and others".

(*Qf&p* 7.02)

The same principles apply: firstly that the leading is recognised to be a true spiritual calling. As the Friends bringing the concern, we will have done whatever we can to deepen our understanding of the

---

6   Personal communication

issues. We ask for the meeting's further discernment as to whether it is a concern, or a new expression of concern, that is core to Quakers in Britain. Perhaps it is a response to a situation that is widespread and not confined to one area. It could be a piece of work that we are willing to undertake on behalf of the yearly meeting, but want to know that we have that support. We might need the expertise of staff or of Friends in other meetings, or want to make connections with them. Just as when we tested it in the area meeting, we may need to differentiate between the concern itself and the course of action proposed. In 2016 several area meetings, having done all they could locally, sent minutes of concern about forced migration to Meeting for Sufferings. It united with the concern, but was less clear about what Friends corporately are called to do in a complex and changing situation. The outcome has been the creation of a new staff post to scope and develop ideas for effective action. Meanwhile QARN (Quaker Asylum & Refugee Network) continues to channel and support Friends' energies.

Diana and John Lampen highlight another aspect that is important to consider: "…local Friends may be very willing to commend the spiritual integrity of one of their members; but they often lack the expertise to evaluate whether the Friend has the necessary skills and whether the work is actually needed, practical, unlikely to do harm, and wanted by the recipients" (Lampen and Lampen, 2006, p. 49). There will always be a tension between recognising and following a leading and the need for clear planning and to identify measurable outcomes (especially so if we are seeking funding). But "if we were to shut the door on discernment processes which cannot be fully explained in rational terms, we would lose part of the Quaker understanding of concern" (ibid., p. 46).

Where does testimony fit in?

Michael Birkel describes the testimonies as "the enduring ethical principles that shape behaviour", while "a leading is often a specific guidance of divine inspiration that embodies one or more of these principles" (Birkel, 2013, p. 247).

In his 1996 Swarthmore Lecture Jonathan Dale finds testimony to be "the corporate working out of our faith". He says, "What BYM's corporate concern [about housing] does is to gather up and refocus all that spiritual energy from all our attempts to put our testimonies into practice." For him, "An individual concern is an individual or small group under concern, carrying through a piece of work which results from a direct calling", while "A corporate concern… is a position adopted by the Society to try to move our own lives and the political process in the direction of our testimonies. It needs to be grounded in the lives of Friends who have worked actively on the issue. It looks towards limited forms of action from large numbers of Friends" (Dale, 1996, pp. 96–97). This is helpfully clear, but I think misses a sense of interchange, of mutual spiritual nourishment. Those "limited forms of action" are not imposed on or required of us, but themselves spring from individual responses to a spiritual call. Without those responses, it would cease to be a genuine communally held concern.

An example might be opposition to the Trident nuclear missile system. Our peace testimony underpins our tested and long-held concern to rid the world of nuclear weapons, and the leadings of individual Friends. They all feed each other. We worship and sing and hold vigils; we chain ourselves together at Faslane and Burghfield; we are moved to campaign and write and speak out and demonstrate. We risk arrest. Other leadings – involvement in peace education or conflict resolution, opposition to the arms trade – contribute to our enduring witness to peace. All that spiritual energy feeds the testimony from which it springs. If that commitment is no longer evident, the testimony will founder.

Concerns adopted by the yearly meeting will draw more of us in, but may not carry everyone along. In 2011 Meeting for Sufferings noted in its minute on Boycott, Divestment and Sanctions (Israel–Palestine): "Although we unite in this decision, we recognise that Friends have different views, and we must treat one another tenderly" (MfS/11/04/4). Sometimes concerns take wing and spread into the wider culture, developing a life of their own. Beth Allen writes about the development of the peace tax concern (withholding the portion of tax designated for military expenditure). From being perceived as a hopelessly idealistic gesture it became supported by the yearly meeting, which tested the law in the courts on behalf of some BYM staff. "This concern met all our tests. The two crucial ones, it seems to me, are first that it nagged at us… and secondly that when we pulled the string, it kept on coming. There was a next step we could take. So we went on keeping the idea alive, and eventually the idea grew its own separate organisation, Conscience – the Peace Tax Campaign – and the initiative passed to others" (Allen, 2007, p. 35). As I write, the Private Members' Bill introduced by Quaker MP Ruth Cadbury – Income Tax (Non-Military Expenditure) Bill 2016–17 – has just been granted its second reading in the Westminster parliament. Other examples of concerns developing a life of their own are Campaign Against Arms Trade, which Quakers helped to set up in 1974, the Alternatives to Violence Project, and Circles of Support and Accountability. All of these show "the hallmarks – a small project, faithfully followed, where our first initiative moved to a different level…" (Allen, 2007, p. 35).

CHAPTER 9

Why share? Why not?

"The importance of the local worshipping group in fostering active concerns cannot be over-emphasised. Where Friends know and trust one another the gifts we all have can be used more fully in obedience to the Inward Light. This is the source from which concerns spring."

Quaker faith & practice 13.09

We may be understandably hesitant in bringing our leading or concern to our meeting: we may feel that we should not be taking up the meeting's time, or that other people are doing far more important things than we are. There may simply be no opportunities, apart from asking for it to come to a business meeting as an agenda item – and we may not feel ready for that. Perhaps we feel a separation between our shared worship and what we do outside of that. But we might find that Friends are pleased that we trust them to hear our experience and are glad to offer help and encouragement.

In her 1997 Swarthmore Lecture *Previous convictions*, Christine Trevett provides a vivid image: "For Isaac Penington the gathered group was the fire itself, with Quakers 'an heap of living coals warming one another'. Coals together release heat, light, energy. Removed from their place in the hearth and laid out individually they quickly lose their power" (Trevett, 1997, p. 108). And new coals catch fire from those already blazing. Ways may open to develop our leading more fully, which we could not have anticipated. In *Minding the future* Christine Davis writes about the sense of being upheld in demanding tasks undertaken under concern rather than from a sense of obligation: "Many other Friends have experienced the same support for a tested concern; others may not have done so, through diffidence about bringing their concerns to the Meeting or through the inattentiveness of the Meeting to what they may be longing, yet feel inadequate, to do. We cannot afford to waste our resources in such a way" (Davis, 2008, p. 84).

VOICES

Why keep it to yourself?

What business is it of my meeting?
It never occurred to me to involve my meeting: I'll just tell them
I'll be away for a few months.

We don't want to bother the meeting.
Everyone's so busy – there's no time.

I wouldn't know how [to share it with my meeting].

Am I committed enough?

It's not in STEPS [an acronym for the Quaker testimonies].

We seem to have less experience of testing concern at all
levels, from personal, through local and area meetings. Many
individuals are acting on their leadings, but rarely doing it as a
tested concern.

At Yearly Meeting 2016 I reported on responses to a Meeting for Sufferings survey from area meetings about tested concerns and corporate action. I noted that respondents to the survey reported 116 times in total that they knew of Friends acting under concern individually. My report went on to say, "It wasn't clear how many of them had asked their Meeting to test or support the leading that they felt. Are we perhaps not always willing to share what impels us to act? Or are we sometimes reluctant to submit to the discipline of testing by the Meeting? Our Friends in Junior Yearly Meeting urge us not to be afraid of the Light and how it may push us. We need not be afraid either of sharing that experience with our Meeting. It may give us, at the very least, loving support when we need it, and may itself be moved to engage with our concern and amplify our efforts."

Those 116 Friends (and no doubt more) have been much on my mind. The respondents to the survey do at least know that they are

engaged in some kind of Quaker-related activity, and some of them
will be actively involved in a tested concern of the meeting. But from
where do they draw strength, if not from their meeting? In her poem
Outside the Baker's Helen Farish writes about…

> "being given what you wanted: cakes, bread,
> light you hadn't reckoned on like a blessing
> you didn't know you needed."

(Farish, 2005)

The loving support, interest and encouragement of a meeting might
be that blessing.

CHAPTER 10

Something should be done

"Matters which we are 'concerned about' are often very important. They might include changing the way that Britain Yearly Meeting does something or hoping that it will undertake a particular service."

Quaker faith & practice 13.01

For many years I had a postcard pinned above my desk. It was a cartoon of a family slumped in front of the TV news. The caption read: "Why don't they DO something?" I often feel like that. In her 1994 Swarthmore Lecture Margaret Heathfield writes, "Imagine a Friend bringing a traditional concern in the traditional way: 'I feel led to do something about this issue, Friends, and I need you to help me to see whether this leading is from God. If you agree that I am so led, I would value your support, because if I am doing that, I may not be able to do anything else.' This is different in a crucial way from a Friend who says 'I feel we should get something done about such and such.' The response 'I hope that will be done' usually infers… '*by others*'" (Heathfield, 1994, p. 80).

Many Friends who are in touch with current affairs will be at times disappointed, frustrated and angry at what seems like a world gone wrong. Sometimes we hear them say, "Quakers should be taking the lead", or "We need to organise ourselves better – we can't just rely on the Spirit to move us." Ministry at a recent Yearly Meeting included the comment, "I have lots of concerns but I don't have time to deal with them."

These are not concerns personally experienced as an inward calling. Does that mean they are insignificant and can be dismissed out of hand? Not necessarily. These 'concerns-about' have their own importance. Underlying the words may be distress, anxiety, guilt or fear, which could well be shared by others in our meeting. "Why doesn't someone take action?" might be a cry of despair or a question – "What can *we* do to make things better?" We might need to look deeper and listen more carefully – we need to pay attention.

Elders and overseers have a particular responsibility here. At a time of sudden disaster or a troubling event, it could be helpful to set aside a time to grieve together. Making time for sorrow can allow us to take stock together and consider what love now requires of us.

It can be difficult to deal with the pressure of what can seem like a tsunami of problems. We all need to find ways to balance the urgency of demands on our attention against true urges of the Spirit. Could the meeting arrange a workshop to explore ways of handling the barrage of news and opinion that comes our way every day, or how we use social media wisely? We can all feel a dissonance between the needs of the world and our own capacity to help: perhaps we could ask a small group to collate local volunteering opportunities.

When there is national upheaval and division, the meeting can be a safe space to express feelings. Just before the 2014 Scottish independence referendum, my area meeting held an extended worship-sharing exercise. We spoke of our visions of the country we wanted to live in. Ministry was heartfelt, moving and often profound. Friends on both sides, and the undecided, were able to express their doubts, fears and hopes in the knowledge that they were heard.

CHAPTER 11

The day of small things

"We must look to ourselves, to speak of our lives and to let our lives speak."

Quaker faith & practice 29.02

Two of the most-used expressions in our Quaker world are "that of God in every one" (*Qf&p* 19.32) and "let your life speak" (*Advices & queries* 27). We may not have credal statements, but together these phrases contribute to an implicit, unformulated creed. Perhaps 'tenets' is a useful concept here – principles that we hold to be true.

I do not believe that letting our lives speak is an injunction not to speak about our lives. I understand it as a reminder that our behaviour must be congruent with what we say we believe. *Advices & queries* 27 continues: "…are you ready to join with others in seeking clearness, asking for God's guidance and offering counsel to one another?" It could be said that we will only do this well when we know each other well. But what better way to know each other well than by being willing to speak of our lives and how we try to live our faith? Like Christine Davis, I believe that "we need to do more to share our experience of being 'love in action' for our neighbours and friends and for those we pass in the street" (Davis, 2008, p. 31). Her wording is important: not just what we do, but "our experience of being". It does not matter what images or language we use – we are the only ones who know how it feels to us.

Do we need to bring every small prompting, what Mathilda Navias calls "everyday leadings", to our meeting to be tested (Navias, 2012, p. 119)? Of course not. But sharing them might be a means to help build true community, a community that practises listening and is prepared to be both excited and challenged. Jonathan Dale offers a warning: "[Our community] is strong enough to create ties of friendship, but not strong enough to challenge us into more faithful discipleship" (Dale, 1996, p. 99). He goes on: "Our individualism prevents our learning from each other… we are afraid of such sharing – it might make demands on us. We claim to be open to God's guidance, but we close up if it comes through that of God in another Friend. We have not created a culture of mutual encouragement and of keen stimulation" (ibid., p. 94).

A meeting that does not make space and time for Friends to talk about how they express their faith in unremarkable ways may find itself ill-equipped to test a more significant leading or concern. It might feel that collectively it has neither the skill nor the spiritual authority to do this work and find it uncomfortable and challenging. But a meeting already practised in sharing the everyday expressions and dilemmas of our faith will be better prepared. There will be a natural reticence, and I expect that many of us feel sympathy with the opening lines of a song lyric by Bulat Okudzhava: "Let us not boast of our righteous lives/Let us go home quietly tonight." But this is not about us and our achievements; it is about finding ways to share, in all humility, how the Spirit leads us.

A story of my own experience of a prompting: On 9/11 I was protesting at an arms fair in London. On 12 September I was waiting to fly home from Heathrow. Watching the planes taking off and landing in tightly controlled patterns, I was suddenly aware of what had been required of air traffic controllers the day before – to return all planes headed for the USA and get them landed safely, without further catastrophe. I was filled with admiration for what must have entailed extraordinary coolness under pressure, and hours of exhausting concentration. When I reached home I had a powerful sense that I must write to say, "Well done and thank you."

I imagined the letter would either not reach the right person, or would be lost amongst many such expressions of appreciation. Ten days later to my surprise I received a personal reply. Steve, the general manager, told me how much my message had meant to him. He wrote that they did not have a contingency plan for "the closure of North America", and praised the fantastic job that his colleagues had done. He had circulated the letter to all the controllers involved. Reading it had "genuinely lifted my spirits after a very dispiriting week".

Since then I have tried to take every opportunity I can to say, "Well done and thank you" to people whose work behind the scenes we take for granted.

Voices

Sharing our stories

Our personal spiritual lives if nourished will seep out into the world.

Meetings that are spiritually alive are moved to live out their faith in the world.

If more Friends bring their leading to meeting, it will support them, and it will give meetings the practice they need.

The Friend who regularly takes part in vigils and demonstrations against nuclear weapons, who recognises that her faith now requires her to break the law. The new attender whose workplace ethos is in conflict with his commitment to honesty. The parent trying to balance her children's need for acceptance by their peers with her fears about the influence of social media. The teenager who refuses to attend an army recruitment presentation at school. The Friend who tells us about her leading to change her job to one that is less secure but more socially useful. By sharing their stories, they take the meeting to the place where faith and practice meet, and in doing so enrich and deepen its life. This is a meeting that will be a source of strength for the Friend who is struck with the horror of a situation and turns her life upside down to spend it with the homeless.

Christine Davis sees us as stewards of our testimony and of all the resources we hold, including the words we use and our spiritual practices. "If we are to be alive as a Quaker group, we need to build trust, understanding and mutual confidence" (Davis, 2008, p. 45). How many of us (I know I am one) have felt strongly led to attend a course at Woodbrooke or elsewhere? We were sure that it would benefit both us and our meeting. On our return we have been disappointed to meet with only mild interest, if that. Could it be because we were reluctant to share that leading beforehand? Would a meeting that feels part of the story feel more engaged, that we were doing this for everyone? This meeting might actively seek to benefit, providing opportunities for us to share what we have learnt, and seeing it as a way of building the life of the community.

A Friend asks, "Do we have some precious and powerful tools languishing in a rusty toolkit? Do we really know how to use them?" A lot has been written about creating resilient communities – resilient against sudden disaster or long-term threats like climate change. Fundamental to the concept of resilience is the need to be prepared. One way that I try to make myself prepared for small domestic emergencies is by having a well-stocked toolbox – and knowing how to find it in the dark. But resilience also includes being prepared simply for the unexpected: in Quaker terms, for being opened to new light.

What are these "precious and powerful tools"? We have the tools of the Spirit: "love, and peace, and tenderness… and helping one another up with a tender hand" (*Qf&p* 10.01). We have our meetings for worship. We have the skill of discernment. We have images, and we have language: we have words towards the unnameable. We sometimes hear it said that we expect people to learn about Quakerism by osmosis, as if Quaker structures and ways of expressing our faith will somehow imperceptibly seep in through mere proximity. If people do not hear the language of everyday faith in practice used, how can it even seep in?

We have other tools – tools for teaching and for learning. When enquirers ask about Quakers, we give them leaflets and a copy of *Advices & queries*, and maybe a list of 'testimonies'. We might sit down with them and talk about what being a Quaker means to us personally. For the rest, we trust to osmosis. But we seem strangely unaware of a most useful teaching tool, which is modelling. Much of what I learnt in my early days as an attender was not from a list of instructions, or from guesswork, but by observing what Quakers did. They stood to minister; they often addressed everyone at the beginning as "Friends"; it was OK to sit quietly in thought at the end of meeting for worship; they said "I hope so" when asked if a minute was acceptable.

If we are to share our experience of trying – and sometimes failing – to be love in action, opportunity and encouragement are both needed. Newer attenders, if they heard us use the language of leadings, might find the window between our worship and our witness less opaque.

Honesty about the challenges of living out our faith might help them (and us) to understand that the Quaker faith is lived out in the "day of small things" – and that there is nowhere it does not apply. Most of us, most of the time, try to be faithful in the ordinary affairs of life rather than in extraordinary acts of courage or witness.

Our elders might encourage this kind of sharing, which I believe would enrich our meetings. There are occasions, less formal than a business meeting, already available to us – house groups, meetings for learning, shared meals. Many meetings now have a short time after meeting for worship that goes under a name like 'afterwords' or 'bridging time'. It is not universally liked, but for some meetings it has become part of the culture, a space to share not-quite-ministry or joys and sorrows. Might sharing our promptings and leadings also be a wise use of this period – both temporally and spiritually, a bridge between our faith and 'the world out there'? Some of us, sometimes, might use these opportunities to share our love-in-action stories – modelling ways to talk about them "without undue pride", and using whatever language best expresses our experience.

As I have written and reflected, I have begun to hope that we might be a bit more adventurous and more trusting in sharing this experience of being moved by the Spirit. If we used our tools of discipline, discrimination and discernment, would we have a few very select 'concerns'? Or would we find our meetings were living, joyful books of love-in-action stories? Becoming more practised in listening and in sharing, we might find that we start to recognise the Spirit moving in each of us, and the confidence to talk about the many and varied expressions of our faith in practice.

Earlier, I used botanical metaphors. I think of the fruits and flowers of our lives as rooted in our worship together, and our meetings as the earth in which the seeds of the Spirit are nourished. Sharing our stories might be a way to help cultivate the soil in which leadings can flourish.

I find myself wanting to say, "Take heed, dear Friends, to the promptings of love and truth in your hearts. Trust them, *and share them*, as the leadings of God whose Light shows us our darkness and brings us to new life."

Stories

The first two stories were given to Yearly Meeting in London in 2016 as invited ministry by Gill Pennington and Lee Taylor. The third is my own story.

Gill Pennington

I was in an A level revision chemistry lesson at Ackworth School when the head teacher came to fetch me. My dad had come up to school to tell my brother and I that my mum had been killed in a road traffic accident the previous evening. Work stopped, my A level results were poor, and instead of going to medical school I studied biology and then became a teacher – the one thing my mum had always advised me not to do, perhaps because she was one herself and knew what hard work it is!

How do we recognise our gifts? Over the next 35 years I honed my teaching skills and added facilitation, coaching and counselling to my toolkit. I had my own 'dark night of the soul', suffering a period of depression when the children left home to go to university, my marriage ended and work became impossible.

For a time, living all alone and comforted only by my beloved border terrier Sam, I was immobilised by mental anguish, wondering if life was worth living at all. Slowly, slowly, I recovered and began to re-engage with the world, starting my own consultancy business, buying my own home, leading a 'Hearts & Minds Prepared' group at meeting. God was preparing me for his work: building my confidence and embedding my gifts.

In 2009, when the recession was at its height and I had very little work, a Friend in my meeting showed me a job advert in *The Friend*. It was at Woodbrooke, which I discovered is the Quaker Study Centre in Birmingham. She said, "You could do that", and on reflection I thought I could! I applied and was invited for interview. Knowing that at interview appearance is important, and being familiar with the business world, I wore my beautiful wool suit and stiletto heels. My hair was up, my make-up on… I looked fabulous! However, as soon as I walked through the front door at Woodbrooke I realised that I had got it all wrong. I felt overdressed and underprepared. Needless to say, they were very kind but I didn't get the job. I fell in love with Woodbrooke though.

The following year I enrolled on 'Equipping for Ministry' (EfM), a two-year, part-time programme. As I went through my first year, immersing myself in the calm tranquillity and enriching teaching that is Woodbrooke, I struggled with what God was saying to me – "Trust me", "Just be". How could I trust God when I had so little income that I wasn't sure where my next meal was going to come from? How could I "just be" when I needed to continuously 'put myself out there' in order to find business? In fact, I didn't ever miss a meal – especially when at Woodbrooke – so I was being cared for.

During my first tutorial my EfM tutor gave me this quotation: "The place God calls you to is the place where your deep gladness and the world's deep hunger meet" (Frederick Buechner). Over the year I began to realise that now I was released from family and regular employment commitments, I was free in a way I had never been before. I could choose to let my whole life be my ministry, and perhaps this would involve working for Quakers…

In January 2011 the Head of Learning at Woodbrooke rang to offer me the job of Tutor for Quaker Roles. I was still driving home from the interview when I got the call, back to my beloved New Forest where I had lived for 30 years.

I accepted at once. We discussed how I could manage the commuting, as I didn't want to move, and I started the following month. My wildest dream had come true – I was working at Woodbrooke. God is amazing!

God also has a sense of humour! My carefully laid plans about how to manage the role and continue living in Hampshire came tumbling down around my ears, and it quickly became very apparent that I was to be in Birmingham. How did I know this? Well, a meeting for clearness helped, as did talking with other EfM-ers and with wise Friends from my meeting. But actually, events overtook me as God picked me up by the scruff of the neck and dumped me in Birmingham. Still during the recession, I sold my home, bought a new one inside a week and moved house in under three months. Who says miracles never happen?

Living in Birmingham is a challenge. I am a country girl through and through and the city overwhelms me. I escape the city when I can but it has taken a long time for my soul to catch up with my physically moved body, and even now there is a sadness within me that I have learned to live with.

I long for the peace of the fields and the trees, the gentle ruminating of cows, the open rides, the pigs and the ponies wandering free, star-laden skies, the sea, long walks, with no traffic noise, clean air and few people. I believe that this is 'the cross' I am called to bear. It sits alongside the deep gladness and joy I feel as I fulfil my ministry and use my gifts in God's service.

God really is amazing! The gifts that God has nurtured through my life are being used and new ones have emerged and grown as I immerse myself in a second role as Spirituality Tutor. This continues: last week I was appointed as Ministry Programmes Coordinator in place of the Quaker roles position I have been holding for the past five years. It seems that as my own spiritual life deepens and matures, I can offer my life in service to God and to Quakers in new ways.

There is also the opportunity to discern and nurture gifts in others – inviting Friends to join our associate tutor team, offering spiritual direction and walking alongside people on courses as they discover their own next steps and consider how to live adventurously.

As I was recovering from depression, a close friend sent me a card with the following words on it:

"When you come to the edge of all that you know
You must believe in one of two things:
There will be earth upon which to stand
Or you will be given wings."

If you are standing on the edge, take the time to discern if now is the time to "live adventurously". If it is, take the risk and step out, putting your faith into action as you are called into a new way of being. It takes courage and it is not easy, but when we take that step, using the gifts we recognise in ourselves or that others have discerned lie within us, we grow spiritually. We deepen our understanding of our true self, discovering more about our connection with the divine and breathing life into our Quaker meetings.

Lee Taylor

In retrospect, I am not sure of the exact timeline, but I do have a crystal-clear recall of the moment I knew I was called to do more to support Quaker work in Matabeleland, Zimbabwe.

Let me describe my experience – a prompting, which I now realise is part of our shared tradition of recognising and then acting under concern.

My friend David Jobson, then at Hlekweni Friends Rural Service Centre near Bulawayo, kept saying to me, "When are you going to come and do some work here?" I finally went in spring 2007 and learned a great deal – it was a time when inflation was mega, there was little food or fuel to be had, and people were struggling. Central and Southern Africa Yearly Meeting met at Hlekweni, and, to be honest, my month was mainly exhilarating, despite the (relative) hardships of living there.

I went back in 2009 and again saw poverty, hunger, the consequences of AIDS. This time, the aftermath was very tough: I think I was soul-sick on my return. What is our world like to tolerate such inequalities? How could I continue my life here in the same way? What could I, or any small group, do?

The process of discernment, of uncomfortable-ness, of internal 'nudging' was underway. It was not an easy time.

Alongside, in response to wanting to support David's work (and an instruction from our financial examiner), our meeting encouraged the formation of a small charity, Friends of Hlekweni. I was involved, alongside other faithful trustees.

However, my involvement was then directed.

My dog and I were walking round our usual morning circuit. I was not thinking of much at all; the dog was doing her thing. Suddenly, and without warning, I found myself stopped in my tracks by the realisation that I was being asked to do much more. This was both a spiritual and physical experience. I think I shook my head; I know that I turned away and walked back in the meadow, as if I could somehow ignore this call. I then stopped, took a few tentative paces in various directions – the dog was beginning to eye me quizzically by this stage – before another recognition: that I had accepted the call.

This probably all sounds rather woolly, but this was my experience. I knew I had some attributes – gifts? – to bring, but I also had faith that I – we – would be given whatever was needed.

My meeting supports the work of Friends of Hlekweni – we discussed whether it was a 'concern'. (John and Diana Lampen's chapter on Quaker concern in *Endeavours to mend* has been helpful to me – 'concern' is not an easy concept for the Society to grasp.) No meeting for clearness was involved. Elders supported me: on one visit I asked for upholding – a prayer rota was organised and I experienced the palpable power of being upheld when struggling.

I would say the call to service transformed me. I carry with me constantly a sense of being somehow 'alongside' my friends, and the schoolchildren, in Zimbabwe who are struggling with poverty and injustice – currently with hunger. There is much to be said for a 'ministry of presence'. But compassion on its own can be paralysing: what can these hands do as part of God's work? I – and other trustees – wrestle with what Friends of Hlekweni can and can't do. The work here is often routine (boring?) but necessary.

There is a constant challenge to decide whether my time is better spent on my laptop and phone here or 'in the field'. I often muse over why I am being asked to work 6,000 miles away: it would have been much easier, God knows, if it'd been closer to home. I try not to 'out-run my Guide', prayerfully asking for guidance.

There have been abundant joys and blessings involved in the service: being part of a longstanding Quaker commitment to work in this area of Zimbabwe; getting to know others "in the things which are eternal" (sharing long, hot, bumpy journeys in a bakkie gets one very close to others); trying to 'walk a mile' in another's shoes; numerous small acts of faith; worshipping with the much smaller Central and Southern Africa Yearly Meeting; travelling 'in the ministry' with another companion; appreciating new friendships; being thankful for the huge generosity of Friends. These – usually – take me through the times of struggle.

I am far more conscious of my own use of the world's resources, particularly food.

How will I know when and if God wishes me to lay down this concern? I don't know. I continue to trust in the process of discernment and openness to the workings of the Spirit revealed to me in a meadow while walking my dog.

ℭ

My own story

It was 1999. A meeting of my local Churches Together group. I was sitting in an armchair in the corner of someone's living room. There was a window on my left. The wallpaper was pale green. I believe this is a fairly common experience, remembering details of the scene just before one's life changes its course. We were discussing what the churches would do to commemorate the millennium. I had been listening with a mounting sense of frustration to plans for services and celebrations.

"We need to change the world," I found myself saying. "I want to be able to tell my grandchildren that we made a difference."

I can honestly say that when I started to speak I had no idea what I was going to say. I heard myself telling the assembled clerics about the horrors of landmines and other remnants of war contaminating land after conflict. I told them how it prevented people, sometimes for generations, from living a normal, fear-free life. I had a little knowledge of this because I supported a small demining agency, MAG (Mines Advisory Group), among other good causes. That's all it had been up until that moment – another good cause. I had not prepared anything. I began: "Why don't we…?"

Where did it come from? I was as surprised as anyone in the room – not only by what I said, but by the urgency and passion in my voice. It seemed to come from a well deep inside, and at the same time from beyond me. It was ministry. They said yes. Without discussion, without argument. They asked: "What do you need?"

I don't know whether I was stumbling or eloquent, but I have never forgotten that sense of being given words, of being acted upon, and of the certainty that I was being given a task to do. By the end of the evening I'd agreed to run a joint year-long fundraising appeal. The theme was 'Because You Can'… walk across a field without fear, let your children out to play or go to school, travel to the next town.

At the end of the year, I went back and said, "I can't stop now. I've learnt too much. I have to carry on." Again they said, "Yes."

By the end of the third year I'd founded a charity. It was for post-conflict recovery in Cambodia – specifically to support MAG in its work of clearing land after warfare and making it useable for the rural poor. It was a new phase in my life, in which I did things that would previously have frightened me. I haven't stopped since. Sometimes it takes a back seat, but it is always there.

Did I realise at the time that my life would change from that moment, that I would be challenged to go well beyond my comfort zone and beyond any competencies I thought I had? It is easy with hindsight to say yes, but I don't believe I did. I had to learn how to fundraise (I'd never done anything like it before); become a public speaker (it terrified me); a lobbyist (I used to be afraid of being a nuisance); a solo traveller to distant lands; a political activist. I learnt to be hard-headed about finances and disciplined about projects. I have learnt more about the mechanics of killing than I ever wanted to. I have walked in minefields, entrusting my life to people I had just met. I have seen sights, heard stories and experienced situations that have made me cry, and rage, and feel utterly overwhelmed. And I have shared the joy of people whose land has been cleared and whose language now has a future tense – of hopes and plans.

I sometimes wish I'd been asked to do something more 'Quakerly' and requiring less familiarity with explosive devices. But there it is.

How does this relate to my Quaker life? I was already a Friend (hence the Churches Together meeting) but I was new enough not to be well up on Quaker terminology. The word 'concern' was certainly not one that was current in my then rather sleepy meeting. I told them the story. It never occurred to me to call this story of mine a concern, nor did I ask for it to be adopted, or endorsed, or forwarded. They wished me well, told me it was a good thing and they were pleased I was doing it. I had wanted more but I couldn't articulate what, even to myself. I think I wanted them to catch fire, to feel what I had felt. They didn't, and I was disappointed.

Looking back, I realise with some shame that my meeting unconsciously – and unselfconsciously – provided me with exactly what I needed at the time. Quiet encouragement, an unspoken recognition that something had changed in me, that I had been acted upon in a way I couldn't explain. They gave me love, support, a constant willingness to listen to 'the story so far', and, when I asked, small amounts of money. (This enabled me to buy Cambodian craft goods, often made by mine survivors, to sell on my return – sometimes to the Friends who'd given me the money in the first place. They didn't seem to mind.)

Now I recognise what I experienced (and continue to experience) as a leading. Would it have made any difference had I been more familiar with chapter 13 of *Quaker faith & practice*? Would it have been different if I'd called it a capital-c Concern? Yes, I think it would – and not in a helpful way. I expect it would have been passed on to my monthly [area] meeting, and possibly then to Meeting for Sufferings, which would have sent it to Friends House for advice. None of which would have been necessarily very useful. I take it as a given that most Friends are supportive of the work. It is causally related to our testimony against war, although we would not be starting from here. It is a practical, technical problem, and not a new one. It is not an area where we can contribute corporately, or one that is distinctively Quaker. A Friend in my current area meeting said to me recently, "But you are acting under concern, aren't you? We recognise that." If you like, in following my leading, I am acting under a concern about warfare already held by Friends. Another leaf on the oak tree. I don't act for Quakers; I am a Quaker who is led to act in this way. I no longer yearn for a conflagration. I am content to be a single candle, protected and sheltered by the loving support of Friends.

Bibliography

1 Corinthians 12:4–7. *Revised English Bible* (1997). Oxford: Oxford University Press.

Advices & queries (2008). London: The Yearly Meeting of the Religious Society of Friends (Quakers) in Britain.

Allen, B. (2007). *Ground and spring: foundations of Quaker discipleship* (Swarthmore Lecture). London: Quaker Books.

Barnett, C. (2016, 1 July). 'A shared language', in *The Friend*, p. 14. London: The Friend Publications Limited.

Birkel, M. (2013). 'Leadings and discernment', in S.W. Angell and B.P. Dandelion (eds.), *The Oxford Handbook of Quaker Studies*. Oxford: Oxford University Press.

Book of Christian discipline of the Religious Society of Friends in Great Britain (1883). Yearly Meeting. Ch IV Sect. 11/6. London: Samuel Harris & Co.

Buechner, F. (1993). *Wishful Thinking: A Seeker's ABC* (revised and expanded edition). New York: HarperCollins Publishers.

Christian practice: Being the second part of Christian discipline of the Religious Society of Friends in Great Britain (1925). London: The Friends' Bookshop.

Dale, J. (1996). *Beyond the spirit of the age: Quaker social responsibility at the end of the twentieth century* (Swarthmore Lecture). London: Quaker Home Service.

Dandelion, P. (2007). *An introduction to Quakerism*. Cambridge: Cambridge University Press.

Davis, C.A.M. (2008). *Minding the future* (Swarthmore Lecture). London: Quaker Books.

Dawes, J., ed. (2013). *The Q-bit: at the heart of a Quaker-led organisation. An inquiry into our Quaker identity by the trustees of Quaker Social Action*. London: Quaker Social Action.

Farish, H. (2005). *Intimates*. London: Jonathan Cape.

Gross, Z. (2015). *With a tender hand: a resource book for eldership and oversight*. London: Quaker Books.

Heales, B.C. and C. Cook (1992). *Images and silence: future of Quaker ministry* (Swarthmore Lecture). London: Quaker Home Service.

Heales, B.C. and C. Cook (2004). 'Seeds of the Spirit', in M.P. Abbott and P.S. Parsons (eds.) *Walk worthy of your calling: Quakers and the traveling ministry*. Richmond, IN: Friends United Press.

Heathfield, M. (1994). *Being together: our corporate life in the Religious Society of Friends* (Swarthmore Lecture). London: Quaker Home Service.

Kane, P. (2016, 2 July). www.thenational.scot/comment/19497. Accessed July 2016.

Lampen, D. and J. Lampen (2006). 'Quaker concern', in B. Phillips and J. Lampen (eds.) *Endeavours to mend: perspectives on British Quaker work in the world today*. London: Quaker Books.

Navias, M. (2012). *Quaker process for Friends on the benches*. Philadelphia: Friends Publishing Corporation.

Okudzhava, B. and V. Frumkin (1980). *65 songs (65 pesen)*. Ann Arbor, MI: Ardis Publishing.

Quaker faith & practice: the book of Christian discipline of the Yearly Meeting of the Religious Society of Friends (Quakers) in Britain (fifth edition, 2013). London: The Yearly Meeting of the Religious Society of Friends (Quakers) in Britain.

Routledge, J. (2014). *Living eldership: a journey of discovery*. London: Quaker Books.

Trevett, C. (1997). *Previous convictions and end-of-the-millennium Quakerism* (Swarthmore Lecture). London: Quaker Home Service.

Wilsher, B. and J. Wilsher (1986). 'Origins of Q-PAC', in (Yearly Meeting Agenda Committee) *The nature and variety of concern: the report of a working party*. London: Quaker Home Service.

Wilson, R.C. (1949). *Authority, leadership and concern: a study in motive and administration in Quaker relief work*. London: George Allen & Unwin Ltd.

Yearly Meeting Agenda Committee (1986). *The nature and variety of concern: the report of a working party*. London: Quaker Home Service.